LOST GODDESSES OF
EARLY GREECE

LOST GODDESSES OF EARLY GREECE

A Collection of Pre-Hellenic Myths

With a new Preface

CHARLENE SPRETNAK

BEACON PRESS
BOSTON

Grateful acknowledgment is made for permission to quote from the following: *Persephone: Three Essays on Religion and Thought in Magna Graecia* by Gunther Zuntz, Copyright © 1971, reprinted by permission of Oxford University Press; *The Masks of God: Primitive Mythology* by Joseph Campbell, Copyright © 1959, reprinted by permission of The Viking Press; *The Greek Myths* by Robert Graves, Copyright © 1955, reprinted by permission of A. P. Watt Ltd.; *Prolegomena to the Study of Greek Religion* by Jane Ellen Harrison, Copyright © 1903, 1922, reprinted by permission of University Books, Inc.

First published as a Beacon Paperback in 1981 by special arrangement with Charlene Spretnak; new editions published by Beacon Press in 1984 and 1992. Originally published by Moon Books of Berkeley, California, in 1978.

Book Design: Ann Flanagan
Typesetting: Ann Flanagan Typography, Berkeley, California
Illustrations: Drawings of Minoan and Mycenaean seal stones (round) and gold seal rings (oval), all circa 1500 B.C., by Patricia Reis (The Goddess depicted in each seal expresses the themes in the myth that follows, but is not necessarily the same Goddess named in that myth.)

Beacon Press books are published under the auspices of the Unitarian Universalist Association of Congregations.

Printed in the United States of America

99 98 97 96 95 94 93   8 7 6 5 4 3 2

Library of Congress Cataloging in Publication Data

Spretnak, Charlene, 1946–
    Lost goddesses of early Greece: a collection of pre-Hellenic myths:
with a new preface / Charlene Spretnak.
      p. cm.
    Originally published: Berkeley, Calif.: Moon Books, c1978.
    Includes bibliographical references.
    ISBN 0-8070-1343-9
    1. Goddesses, Greek. 2. Mythology, Greek. I. Title.
BL782.S66 1992
292.2'114 — dc20   91-41829
                                        CIP

for our foremothers
from the beginning

Contents

Preface
to the 1992 Edition

The Return of the Goddess

I am sometimes told that this book was "ahead of its time." That may be true, but it seems to me that the book was evoked, rather mysteriously, by its time. Quite unaware of each other's efforts, a few writers independently had begun the research and writing that led to the first wave of Goddess books: *When God Was a Woman* by Merlin Stone (published first in England in 1975, then in the United States in 1976), *Lost Goddesses of Early Greece* (1978), and *The Spiral Dance* by Starhawk (1979). I do not believe that any of us knew at that time of Marija Gimbutas's pioneering archaeological study, *Goddesses and Gods of Old Europe, 6500–3500 B.C.* (1974). The creation of these works and others in the late seventies did not initiate the rebirth of Goddess spirituality, merely its manifestation in books. Artists such as Mary Beth Edelson and Donna Henes were already working with Goddess themes, *WomanSpirit* magazine was issued quarterly, and workshops were being offered by such early recoverers of Goddess spirituality as Hallie Austen Iglehart and Z. Budapest — but why was interest in this topic bubbling up all around the country?

While there is no simple answer to that question, it is clear that the flowering of Goddess spirituality in the mid-seventies did not grow from a vacuum. It emerged from the rich cultural compost that remained from the social challenges of the previous decade. From the overtly political dimension of the sixties, participants carried forth an awareness of power dynamics and structures of domination. Indeed, turning such an analysis on the alternative political forms of the sixties themselves had resulted in the break-away development of the "second wave" of American feminism, as the phenomenon of consciousness-raising circles spread throughout the land. Viewing patriarchal religious institutions anew with attention to machinations of domination similarly prompted a large-scale exodus and search for alternatives.

From the countercultural dimension of the sixties came an additional political challenge to deeply held assumptions of the status quo. A range of exploratory experiences had peeled back the tightly proscribed "normalcy" of the fifties to reveal an unimagined richness and depth of being. I do not believe that the ancient images of Goddess spirituality, so radically body-honoring and nature-oriented, would have struck such a responsive chord if we had come upon them with the buttoned-down mentality of the fifties. The possibilities suggested by those evocative images most likely would have seemed beyond the reach of women still socialized to be thoroughly "modern." As it was, however, certain experiential awakenings lingered in the air even into the mid-seventies: the honoring of the body; the revelation of an expansive spirituality; the realization of our embeddedness in nature and the dynamics of the cosmos; the liberty of nonrigid, egalitarian social forms; and the confidence to create such forms and practices according to personal and communal needs, dreams, and desires. Granted, the expression of those explorations had often been trivial — or at least trivialized as the sixties had peaked and wound down — but not when they reemerged several years later in the hands of some "serious ladies" who found themselves on a mission. Few among us failed to grasp the sacred charge involved in rescuing from oblivion perhaps the oldest religious tradition of humankind — and, in the process, saving our lives.

The reemergence of Goddess spirituality has never been a simple attempt to reinstate the Goddess religion of the neolithic era, about which we have limited knowledge. Rather, the contemporary movement is based on creative expressions of continuity with the cultural presence of the Goddess, which has existed for some twenty-five thousand years. The Goddess is regarded as a potent metaphor for both the immanence of the divine and the transcendence that is the larger reality, the sacred whole. By "the divine" I mean creativity in the universe, or ultimate mystery — the self-organizing dynamics through which trillions of microevents are manifested each moment throughout the entire cosmos, including our own bodies. The extremely widespread appeal of this spiritual orientation resides not in the composted soil from which it took new life but in the content of the new form itself: the contemporary renaissance of ritual arts of the Earthbody and the personal body, the creative participation in gestalt fields of myth and symbol that are both ancient and elemental, the embodied recognition of the dignity of the female, the active concern about wisdom and justice in the Earth community, and the beckoning lifelong path of unfolding and transformation.

Goddess spirituality activates modes of creativity that draw strength from the profound relatedness of all life, rather than being individualist or collectivist strikes against one's context. The grand adventure that is the unfolding of the person is then recognized as a process of the unfolding story of the Earth community and the cosmos. Engagement with the Goddess in symbol, myth, and ritual *as participatory fields of relation* encourages the expression of one's unique gifts while evoking a sense of one's larger self, the fullness of our being. It is an aesthetic path to grace.

The telling of myth is a ritual creation of sacred space. Reading a myth to oneself or hearing it spoken in a ritual setting draws one's consciousness into a field of relationship that places all participants — the engaged witness, the narrator, the principals of the sacred story — in deep accord with the life processes of the unfolding universe. Myth is sacred narrative evoked by a totemic presence, a manifestation or empowered bearer of cosmic energies. The more a narrative evolves in elaborations distant from the totemic presence, the more it loses vitality and may fade in time to formulaic allegory. The sacred stories of the Goddess are replete with such totemic animals — bears, owls, serpents, deer, and spiders — but clearly the remarkable allure of Goddess myths in disparate eras and cultures results from the fact that the body of the Goddess is itself a totemic presence.

A woman raised in a patriarchal culture is told that she has the wrong type of body-mind to be taken seriously and to share a sexual sameness with God. Patriarchal socialization tells her that the elemental power of the female is somewhat shameful, dirty, and downright dangerous if unrestrained. Imagine, then, the ontological revolution that occurs within such a woman who immerses herself in sacred space where various manifestations of the Goddess bring forth the Earthbody from the spinning void, bestow fertility on field and womb, ease ripe bodies in childbirth, nurture the arts, protect the home, guard one's child against forces of harm, issue guidance for a community, join in ecstatic dance and celebration in sacred groves, and set love's mysteries in play. The woman's possibilities are evoked with a joyous intensity. *She* will create the ongoing completion of each mythic fragment. *She* is in and of the Goddess. *She* will embody the myth with her own totemic being. *She* is the cosmic form of waxing, fullness, waning: innocent virgin, mature creator, wise crone. She cannot be negated ever again. Her roots are too deep — and they are everywhere.

I could scarcely anticipate the full measure of renewal that was to occur through Goddess spirituality when I spoke of *possibilities* at the end of the introduction to the original edition of this book in 1978. My rather modest goal was to set the record straight historically (in the research sections preceding each myth) and to reconstruct the pre-Olympian sacred stories. I knew from personal experience while immersing myself in the research and consciousness of the mythic presence of the Goddess that the recovery of this spirituality was deeply transformative — but how many women would be inclined to participate in that recovery? The answer, eventually, was hundreds of thousands.

Over the years *Lost Goddesses of Early Greece* has found appreciative readers with regard to both its political function of reclaiming stolen history and its spiritual function of illuminating a sacred tradition. It has been invited into educational forums, the performing arts, and the arts of ritual.

In the area of education, I have truly enjoyed hearing accounts of young women, from junior high school through college, taking this book into classrooms to counter the mistaken teachings that the Olympian myths, with their degraded forms of the pre-Hellenic goddesses, were the oldest religion in ancient Greece. Often the young women had received the book as a birthday present, an assist in coming-of-age. *Lost Goddesses of Early Greece* also had the good fortune of being included in the adult curriculum of religious studies produced by the national office of the Unitarian Universalist Association in 1986; two of the pre-Hellenic myths are incorporated in *Cakes for the Queen of Heaven: A Ten-Session Adult Seminar in Feminist Thealogy*, designed by the Reverend Shirley Ann Ranck. That course has been taught in scores of Unitarian Universalist churches around the country and in other denominations as well.

One particular educational presentation of the myths included the performing arts. The physicist and cosmologist Dr. Brian Swimme and I offered a workshop entitled "The Cosmology of the Goddess" at the conference on Ecofeminist Perspectives: Culture, Nature, Theory held in March 1987 at the University of Southern California. We set out to explore cosmologically oriented wisdom in two kinds of knowing: pre-Hellenic mythology and contemporary science. Our pattern was my explaining the pre-Olympian history of one of the myths and then delivering a reading of it, followed by Swimme's exploring a theme suggested in the sacred story.

For our first round, I spoke of the original nature of Aphrodite and gave a reading of her myth. Swimme then spoke on the notion of allurement, the starting point of all the activities in the universe. Musing on the sacred story of Aphrodite's power to activate allurement, he noted that Mach's Principle came to mind, the recognition that everything in the universe is bound together by gravitation, the mysterious attraction or relationship.

For our second round, I spoke of Pandora's original role as the gift-giving maiden form of the Earth Goddess; I then gave a reading of "The Myth of Pandora." Swimme spoke on the unfolding processes of the universe as an act of generosity. A subatomic particle comes into being from nowhere, from a realm of ultimate mystery (similar to the event of Gaia's bringing forth the world from the void). He noted that the supernova explosion is the way the universe shares and disperses its gifts.

For our third round, I spoke about the pre-Olympian nature of Artemis, Selene, and Hecate and then gave a reading of "The Myth of the Triad of the Moon." Swimme proposed that this myth of the triple Goddess suggests a form within which we can think about life and death on this planet. The Earth expresses extraordinary fecundity, such that the ten million species on the planet today are thought to be only 1 percent of all those that have existed here during the past four billion years. Those flourish that fit in well with the interactions of their ecosystem; those that do not are allowed to pass out of the ecocommunity. Life proceeds with astonishing intricacy. He also noted, in explaining his methodology for the workshop, that when he had reflected and meditated on the pre-Hellenic myths until he "became filled with a myth," the ways in which he thought about natural phenomena and even the entire universe were qualitatively different from the perceptions that would have arisen if he had been immersed in, say, the patriarchal, industrialized, competitive, Victorian world that was Darwin's frame of reference. Swimme concluded that the myths have a very deep biological basis and that by allowing ourselves to be filled with a myth, the universe itself is altered because our relationship to the universe is altered in a very real sense.

Perhaps because I tried to remain true to the oral tradition in reconstructing the pre-Olympian myths, their multivalent content has also evoked dramatic productions. A theatrical company named Mother-tongue Theatre performed their moving interpretation of "The Triad of the Moon: Artemis, Selene, Hecate" at the conference on The Great Goddess Re-Emerging, which was held at the University of California at Santa Cruz in April 1978 and coincided with the book's publication. I have also been told of children's groups in Unitarian Universalist churches performing some of the myths in outdoor settings. An additional area of the performing arts is the reading of the myths I have been invited to give, including one on an arts program, "Voices in the Wind," on National Public Radio.

The type of engagement with *Lost Goddesses of Early Greece* that means the most to me is the incorporation of the myths into ritual — personal rituals of one's inner life; women's group rituals of passage and trans-formation; and community rituals of women, men, and children celebrating the solstices and equinoxes. Most of those I will never know of, but my own women's ritual group has used the myth of Hera in a menarche ritual and that of Aphrodite in a prenuptial ritual. In our larger, seasonal ritual gatherings with family and friends, we have incorporated the myth of Demeter and Persephone at the vernal equinox and that of Hecate on the darkest night of the year, winter solstice. When I hear of similar embodiment of the myths in ritual and the recovery of sacred space, I feel deeply grateful for being a part of the process.

One of the most dramatically meaningful ritual en-actments of the pre-Hellenic myths took place in the summer of 1981 on the site of the Telesterion, the Great Hall of Initiation at Eleusis, in Greece. In the early eighties, San Francisco State University spon-sored an Aegean Women's Studies Institute, which included among its faculty Dr. Carol P. Christ and Dr. Mara Lynn Keller. They were joined by another writer on women's spirituality, Patrice Wynne, in en-acting the parts of the narrator, mother, and daughter in "The Myth of Demeter and Persephone" in a ritual that included some sixty women. By their act, the pre-Olympian sacred story of mother and daughter was carried home to the very site of the ancient initiations into the Eleusinian Mysteries of Demeter and Perse-phone.

For many women and men, the significance of re-covering the pre-Hellenic myths is immediately ap-parent. I recall one instance, though, when such awareness took root, in the mind of a renowned male mythologist, only after he happened to hear a woman's deeply felt response. In 1979 Joseph Campbell invited me to join him for lunch during a weekend seminar he was teaching in San Francisco. We sat facing each other, eating sandwiches, at a card table in a room filled with people who were attending the seminar. On the table between us lay a copy of *Lost Goddesses of Early Greece,* which he had heard about but had not yet read. In later years, a friend of his told me, he recommended the book enthusiastically, but that day he was quite nervous and ill at ease. I wondered if his wariness toward me was an uneasy response to his having devoted so little attention to worldwide manifestations of the Goddess in his many books. We had a polite, if somewhat stilted, conversation, at the end of which a woman passing by our table spotted the book and quite spontaneously and joyfully ex-claimed, "That book changed my life!" Her reaction caused Professor Campbell's face to break into ex-pressions of shock and then delight. Perhaps her dec-laration that day helped to spark his belated but respectful attention to the mythology of the Goddess, which he continued for the remainder of his life.

Not knowing I had any connection with the book, the woman had bestowed the ultimate blessing on an author. To learn that one has deeply touched a life negates the memory of long hours of research, the struggles of the creative process, and the sacrifices a major project demands. I experienced her response with palpable waves of both gratitude and awe for the mysterious process at work. On that day I had been given yet another glimpse of the vast and diverse community that was about to emerge, nourished by the power and resilience of the sacred myths of the female, almost lost to us, almost obliterated by denial. What I felt was deliverance.

Acknowledgments

The seeds for this book were planted in the early seventies when I began reading of certain archaeological and anthropological discoveries. In the summer of 1975, I attended a weekend gathering on "Women and Mythology" conducted by Hallie Iglehart. She showed slides of ancient Goddess statues and artifacts from the Mediterranean area and the Near East, and she talked about the numerous clues that indicate an earlier stratum of matrifocal mythology and culture preceded the patriarchal order we call "ancient civilization." I knew of the evidence from my reading, but Hallie's slides and artbooks brought the subject to life. The images stayed with me. The rest of the weekend was spent on explorations into our personal mythology, on recognizing recurring symbols and events, and on seeing in our lives the ancient mythic themes of transformation and rebirth.

The impetus for the book came some three months later when I was riding in our car with my daughter, Lissa Merkel. Her eye was caught by the logo of an oil corporation and she cried, "Look, Mama, a horse with wings!" She became very excited about the idea of a flying horse. I said, "Yes, his name is Pegasus and he's part of a myth. Myths are very, very old stories. Maybe we can find a book of myths in the library and I'll read them to you." Then I drove on farther and thought aloud, ". . . but the oldest ones have been changed." A trip to the public library confirmed what I suspected from my readings in archaeology and anthropology: There were no collections of myths other than engaging editions of Hesiod's and Homer's revisionist works. I went home and took my high school edition of Edith Hamilton's *Mythology* from the shelf. I leafed through it and read that "Zeus had punished men by giving them women"; that Pandora was "that dangerous thing, a woman"; and that from Pandora "comes the race of women, who are evil to men, with a nature to do evil." In the interest of mental health and a positive self-concept, this did not seem the best way to introduce an impressionable, four-year-old girl to the riches of mythology. (Later, while researching the pre-Olympian myths, I discovered that my daughter's name, Lissa, is derived from the Greek *Melissa*, a title for the priestesses of Demeter.)

During the periods of both the research and the writing of this book, my most encouraging and unflagging supporter was my sister, Nikki Spretnak. I also wish to thank Walter Burkert of the University of Zurich, who generously gave his time and advice on the manuscript while he was the Visiting Sather Professor of Classical Literature at the University of California, Berkeley. I am grateful to Michael Gottlieb, Mary Mackey, Valerie Miner, Robin Morgan, Anne

Kent Rush, and Merlin Stone for reading and responding to the original manuscript; Fritjof Capra and Andrew Schmookler offered thoughtful suggestions on the expanded introduction. Daniel Goleman encouraged me to compose my critique of Jungian uses of Greek Goddess mythology and publish it in *Anima*, Fall 1979 (see introduction). Roger Pritchard and Bella Debrida kindly answered my questions about classical Greek. Patricia Reis deserves special thanks for her drawings of the Minoan and Mycenaean seal stones and seal rings (circa 1500 B.C.), as does John K. Anderson, Professor of Classics at the University of California, Berkeley, who aided me in researching the seals. I also wish to acknowledge the efforts of my agent, Frances Goldin, and my editor at Beacon Press, Joanne Wyckoff. Finally, I am fortunate to have received the sustaining support of Ann Flanagan and many others, especially my parents, Donna and Joseph Spretnak.

Charlene Spretnak
Berkeley, California
March 1984

To be gripped by the realization of deity in woman, the spring and harbor of life, mankind did not have to wait for the invention of agriculture. Everywhere, from Spain to Siberia, so many palaeolithic documents of this devotion have emerged, and with traits so specific recurring in neolithic relics, as to forbid the facile inference that this change, however epocal, in man's living habits could by itself account for what is loosely called "the cult of the Mother Goddess"... What evidence there is — and it is not a little — points to concerns more comprehensive and profound. This is the oldest godhead perceived by mankind.

— Gunther Zuntz
Persephone: Three
Essays on Religion
and Thought in
Magna Graecia

There can be no doubt that in the very earliest ages of human history the magical force and wonder of the female was no less a marvel than the universe itself; and this gave to woman a prodigious power, which it has been one of the chief concerns of the masculine part of the population to break, control and employ to its own ends. It is, in fact, most remarkable how many primitive hunting races have the legend of a still more primitive age than their own, in which the women were the sole possessors of the magical art.

—Joseph Campbell
The Masks of God:
Primitive Mythology

The whole of Neolithic Europe, to judge from surviving artifacts and myths, had a remarkably homogeneous system of religious ideas, based on worship of the many-titled Mother-goddess, who was also known in Syria and Libya. Ancient Europe had no gods. The Great Goddess was regarded as immortal, changeless, and omnipotent; and the concept of fatherhood had not been introduced into religious thought.

—Robert Graves
The Greek Myths

The habit of viewing Greek religion exclusively through the medium of Greek literature has brought with it an initial and fundamental error in method. For literature Homer is the beginning, though every scholar is aware that he is nowise primitive... Homer presents, not a starting point, but a culmination, a complete achievement, with scarcely a hint of origines... Beneath this splendid surface lies a stratum... at once more primitive and more permanent.

—Jane Ellen Harrison
Prolegomena to the
Study of Greek
Religion

Introduction

Gaia created the world, Pandora gave bountiful gifts, Artemis led Her worshippers in ecstatic dances, Hera rewarded the girls who ran the first Olympic races, and Athena peacefully protected the home. These Goddesses are among the earliest deities known in Greece, but the original mythology surrounding them has been lost. We know their names only through the relatively late myths of the classical period.

Yet for thousands of years before the classical myths took form and then were written down by Hesiod and Homer in the seventh century B.C., a rich oral tradition of mythmaking had existed. Strains of the earlier tradition are evident in the later myths, which reflect the cultural amalgamation of three waves of barbarian invaders, the Ionians, the Achaeans, and finally the Dorians, who moved into Greece from 2500 to 1000 B.C. These invaders brought with them a patriarchal social order and their thunderbolt God, Zeus. What they found when they entered Greece was a firmly rooted religion of Goddess worship. In various regions of the mainland and the islands, a Goddess was held sacred and was associated with order, wisdom, protection, and the life-giving processes (e.g., seasonal change, fertility of womb and field). Among the Goddesses we know to have preceded the Olympian system are Gaia, Themis, Rhea, Pandora, Aphrodite, Artemis, Leto, Britomaris, Diktynna, Selene, Hecate, Hera, Athena, Demeter, and Persephone.

The invaders' new Gods, the Olympians, differ in many ways from the earlier Goddesses. The pre-Hellenic Goddesses are enmeshed with people's daily experiencing of the energy forces in life; Olympian Gods are distant, removed, "up there." Unlike the flowing, protective love of a Mother-Goddess, the character of the Olympian Gods is judgmental. Olympian Gods are much more warlike than their predecessors and are often involved in strife. The pre-Hellenic Goddesses are powerful and compassionate, yet those whom the Greeks incorporated into the new order were transformed severely. The great Hera was made into a disagreeable, jealous wife; Athena was made into a cold, masculine daughter; Aphrodite was made into a frivolous sexual creature; Artemis was made into the quite forgettable sister of Apollo; and Pandora was made into the troublesome, treacherous source of human woes. These prototypes later evolved into the wicked witch, the cruel stepmother, the passive princess, etc., of our fairy tales. Of all the great Mother-Goddesses, only Demeter survives intact. However, she is not included in the main group on Mount Olympus, in spite of the fact that she is a very old deity and was well known on both the islands and the mainland.

Although the pre-Hellenic Goddesses pre-date considerably the Greek Gods, these Goddesses are relatively late derivatives of the Great Goddess, the supreme deity for millennia in many parts of the world. Her worship seems to have evolved from the awe experienced by our early ancestors as they regularly observed woman's body as the source of life. Paleolithic statues celebrate the mysteries of the female: Woman's body bled painlessly in rhythm with the moon, and her body miraculously *made people,* then provided food for the young by making milk. (In a primitive culture, copulation is not usually associated with the miracle of new life; paternity was not recognized for a long while.) A further mystery to our ancestors was that woman could draw from her body women and men.

Perhaps the earliest Paleolithic statues, dating from 25,000 B.C., are expressions of the female body as living microcosm of the larger experiences of cyclic change, birth, renewal, and nurture. In time these energies became embodied in the sacred presence of the Great Goddess, the encompassing matrix of female power. On her surface she produced food, into her womb she received the dead. Rituals in her honor took place in womb-like caves, often with vulva-like entrances and long, slippery corridors; both the cave entrances and grave sites were often painted with blood-like red ochre, a clay used as pigment. As society evolved, so did the powers of the Goddess. She was revered as the source of life, death and rebirth; as the giver of the arts, divine wisdom, and just law; and as the protector of peace and the nurturer of growth. She was all forces, active and passive, creative and destructive, fierce and gentle.

The Great Goddess was known by many names in many cultures. At various sites of her worship, certain attributes were stressed. Because the traits that were emphasized came to be associated with the local name for the Goddess — and may have been inspired by a particular woman — many derivative forms evolved. The seeming multiplicity of deities is misleading since each was a facet of the one, omnipotent Goddess. Eventually, some of the Goddesses reproduced, always parthenogenetically in prepatriarchal mythology. If the child was a daughter, she joined her mother in administering supernatural powers. If the child was a son, he became his mother's lover and held a subordinate role in the mythology. In graphic representations the son/lover is always pictured as being smaller than the Goddess and is usually in the background. The original perception of the Goddess as the parthenogenetic source of life was still held sacred long after certain biological facts were recognized among her worshippers.

Reclaiming Pre-Hellenic Mythology

The Greek myths of the classical period have long been considered *the* Greek myths. The classicist Jane Ellen Harrison was among the first to recognize that those myths are actually a late development in a long mythic tradition: "Beneath this splendid surface [of Homer's Olympian myths] lies a stratum...at once more primitive and more permanent." Drawing from various sources of evidence, Harrison delineated the strong contrasts between the matrifocal, pre-Hellenic body of mythology and the patriarchal, Olympian system that later evolved.

As successful conquerors, the invaders blended certain aspects of pre-Hellenic religion, i.e., principally the Goddesses' names, with their own patriarchal Gods and themes. For example, Hera had long been associated with the "sacred marriage" — the merging of the lunar cow and the solar bull. However, "sacred marriage" is used in Olympian mythology to refer to Hera's marriage to Zeus. The fact that their union was always a stormy one is thought by many classicists to be a historical reference to the forced merging of the two cultures: Hera is the powerful native queen who is coerced but never subdued by the alien conqueror.

There are a number of reasons why this chapter of our cultural history has been "lost." The most obvious is that the pre-Hellenic myths are the religion of a conquered people, so they were co-opted and replaced for political reasons. Second, pre-Hellenic mythology was an oral tradition, and many of the clues to its nature have been lost over the past 3500 years. Third, a culturally imposed bias among many Victorian and contemporary scholars prevented them from accepting the evidence that deity was originally perceived as female in most areas of the world. In the literature, one never reads of "the religion of Artemis" and "the cult of Jesus"; it is always the other way around. One of the most renowned living mythologists wrote a few years ago that although "paleolithic deposits in Asia and Europe have yielded a great many bone statuettes representing a nude Goddess...we cannot deduce from the *presence* of the paleolithic female statuettes, the *non-existence* of the worship of a divine masculine Being" [his italics]. Similarly, another scholar theorized that the reason numerous Goddess statues are the sole trace of deity during the early Neolithic period on Crete is that the actual supreme deity was probably a male God whose representation was forbidden! If these researchers had dug up numerous statues of male Gods on a remote island, it is extremely unlikely that they would deduce the existence of an unrepresented, supreme "divine feminine Being."

Fortunately for posterity, a number of open-minded classicists and archaeologists have labored to uncover the realities of our pre-Hellenic past. Jane Ellen

Harrison, Marija Gimbutas, Lewis Farnell, Robert Graves, E. O. James, Carl Kerenyi, Martin Nilsson, George Thompson, and R. F. Willetts are among those who have made extensive contributions to our understanding of pre-Hellenic culture and consciousness. Still, much information has been lost concerning pre-Hellenic religion. In order to reconstruct the myths, fragments must be assembled from various sources. One area of evidence is archaeological discoveries. Very early statues, shrines, picture-seals on rings, and labelled figures on ceramic vessels all point to the deeds and rituals associated with various Goddesses. A second area is the writings from the classical period. Homer, Hesiod, Pausanius, Herodotus, Strabo, and others sometimes mentioned, and occasionally recorded rather fully, very old observances of Goddess worship that still took place at certain sites in Greece. A third area is the oral tradition. Many of the stories were preserved among the rustic people; at Ephesus in Anatolia, for instance, the worship of Artemis was kept alive well into the Christian era.

The eleven Goddesses included in this book are those pre-Hellenic deities about whom enough information survived to reconstruct their stories in the original form—that is, before the takeover by the Olympian system of mythology — although certainly no one could presume to reconstruct a long-lost oral tradition exactly. I take full responsibility for the manner in which these myths are written, but the elements and themes are not mine. They have been preserved by the most slender threads from our pre-recorded past. Every symbol, feat, or location associated with the various Goddesses in the myths is based on firm evidence. That is to say, the myths could be footnoted as heavily as are the research introductions, but I felt that such intrusions would violate the artistic integrity of the sacred stories.

The charge can be leveled against the pre-Hellenic myths that they have less plot design, intrigue, and dramatic tension than does Olympian mythology. This is true. Since pre-Hellenic religion flourished and then was crushed before the era of extensive written records, we can hardly do more than piece together portraits of the Goddesses. However, our knowledge of the pre-Hellenic myths, even if incomplete, reveals a compelling alternative to patriarchal cosmology and metaphysics — a more integrated view of life on Earth. As the research for this book proceeded, I came to view my role of conduit as a sacred trust. Although I also write fiction and am not incapable of inventing plots, I chose not to "flesh out" the surviving fragments of evidence beyond the word-smithing necessary to weave the facts together. Moreover, I do not view the pre-Hellenic myths as inert "found objects"; they grew from the collective psyche of our ancestors and are relevant to our own psyches today. My methodology, once the research was completed, was to study all the index cards of information on a particular Goddess, meditate on that material, and then *become* that Goddess as much as possible before reconstructing her myth.

In addition, the pre-Hellenic myths depict a view of life that is quite different from that expressed in the Olympian myths. Even if we had encyclopedic records of the earlier mythology, it seems highly unlikely, judging by what *has* survived, that themes of deceit, treachery, alienation, and brutality informed the pre-Hellenic sacred stories. If such Olympian themes had been embraced by the pre-Hellenic peoples as well, they would have been expressed in the many artifacts and fragments of script. They are not. The pre-Hellenic myths, instead, tell of harmonious bonds among humans, animals, and nature. They express respect for and celebration of the mysteries of body and spirit.

The latest edition of the voluminous *Cambridge Ancient History* deftly notes that various aspects of the pre-Hellenic religion are "under lively discussion." Quite so. It is important that the evidence be aired, that connections be made, that particulars be debated. Yet the essence of these prehistoric myths will be grasped only if we can let go of a protective, supposedly detached pose and enter into the body of myths with openness. If we can succeed in reading these spiritual stories with spiritual perceptions, a sense of continuity with our past may result.

Implications for Patriarchal Religion
and Culture

When compared to the religions of the Goddess in Europe and elsewhere, the Judeo-Christian tradition was "born yesterday." In fact, the very notion of supreme deity, i.e., ultimate power, being male is a relatively recent invention. Zeus first appeared around 2500 B.C., and Abraham, the first patriarch of the Old Testament, is dated by Biblical scholars at 1800 B.C.; in contrast, some of the Goddess statues are dated at 25,000 B.C. Therefore, what we see around us, that is, patriarchal religion and social order, is not "the natural order" for all humankind since Day One based on "the Natural Law."

The new, patriarchal religion co-opted the older mythic symbols and inverted their meaning: The female, Eve, was now weak-willed and treacherous; the sacred bough was now forbidden; and the serpent, symbol of regeneration and renewal with its shedding skins, was now the embodiment of evil. The Goddess religion and its "pagan" worshippers were brutally destroyed in the Biblical lands, just as they had been conquered, co-opted, and destroyed in Old Europe, the Middle East, and India by Indo-European invaders. The Old Testament is the military and cultural record (albeit considerably laundered) of a massive political coup. It is important to note that we did not emerge

into patriarchal religion from a dark, chaotic, im-
mature period of primitivism; Goddess-centered cul-
tures, including Minoan Crete, were highly evolved.
(See *When God Was A Woman* by Merlin Stone and
The Language of the Goddess and *The Civilization of the
Goddess* by Marija Gimbutas.)

In the Christian tradition, the Virgin Mary is
clearly rooted in the older Goddess religion because
she produces her child parthenogenetically. (And Jesus
himself is true to the older pattern of the Goddess'
son/lover dying at the Spring Equinox and being re-
born at the Winter Solstice.) The church co-opted
Mary in order to make converts. She is not included
in the core symbols, i.e., the trinity, but the church
fathers discovered they could not attract followers in
the heavily Goddess-oriented Mediterranean and Celtic
cultures, which then stretched from the Balkans to
the British Isles, without a Goddess on their banners:
Mary, Mother of God, formerly God herself. Far from
"elevating the feminine," the church demoted her,
stripped her of her power, and rendered her docile
and sexless.

The Judeo-Christian tradition has long sought to
eradicate all traces of Goddess religion. The Old Testament is full of references to slaughtering the pagans
and destroying their shrines, yet their presence continued through every Biblical era. On the other side
of the Mediterranean, her worshippers were equally

steadfast. Long into the Christian age, the women of Greece and Anatolia (Turkey) insisted on praying to Artemis in time of childbirth, and the church forcibly closed the last Goddess temple as late as 500 A.D. Many of the Goddess' sacred sites, such as the Parthenon of the Acropolis, were converted into Christian churches. During the Middle Ages, the widespread witch-burnings, a patriarchally approved campaign of mass murder, were largely designed to eliminate independent women who still followed the Old Religion, i.e., worshipped the Goddess in some form, observed nature's holy days (solstices and equinoxes), and practiced herbal healing, abortion, and contraception. In the medieval legends of St. George (the church) slaying the dragon (the huge snake-like symbol of the Old Religion), the dragon's head often grows back. Today a similar wave of rebellion is challenging patriarchal religion. (See *The Spiral Dance: A Rebirth of the Ancient Religion of the Great Goddess* by Starhawk and *Drawing Down the Moon* by Margot Adler.)

Problems with Jungian Uses of Greek Goddess Mythology

There are almost as many interpretations of myth as there are mythologists. Two poles of the spectrum are represented by Robert Graves and Carl Jung. Graves maintains, "Greek mythology was no more mysterious in content than are modern election cartoons."[1] In his two-volume study, *The Greek Myths*, Graves' extensive annotations are a treasury of information on the interplay of matriarchal and patriarchal politics. Jung, in contrast, wrote, "We can hardly suppose that myth and mystery were invented for any conscious purpose; it seems much more likely that they were the involuntary revelation of a psychic, but unconscious, pre-condition."[2] With regard to pre-Olympian mythology specifically, both of these perspectives are valid.

Certainly there are a number of political references in classical mythology to the trauma of occupation by the barbarian invaders. Just as Hera's turbulent marriage to Zeus is thought to be a historical reference, so classicists have proposed that the rape of Persephone reflects the rape of the pre-Hellenic culture and does not seem to have been part of her mythology before the invasions. (In Jungian terms, the rape would be seen as an intrusion of patriarchal consciousness into the earlier matriarchal mode.)

Another example supporting Graves' view is the myth of the rivalry between Athena and Poseidon, which bears clues to a massive societal shift away from pre-Hellenic customs. In a vote by the citizens of Athens, the men voted for Poseidon and the women for Athena. Since the women outnumbered the men by one, Athena won. To appease the wrath of Poseidon, the men inflicted upon the women a triple punishment: They were to lose their vote, their children were no longer to be called by their mothers' name; and they themselves were no longer to be called Athenians after their Goddess.

On the other hand, both pre-Hellenic and classical mythology also abound with references to the psyche. Jung was aware, of course, of the matriarchal stratum of our cultural history. He warned that most myth reflects archetypes only indirectly because the mythological traditions that have survived through long periods of time have "received a specific stamp," have been "submitted to conscious elaboration," and have evolved as a "historical formula."[3] Jung knew that the classical Greek myths, for instance, had been "elaborated" extensively, and he once referred to them as "the hackneyed *chronique scandaleuse* of Olympus."[4] However, he never made a clear, consistent distinction between the two bodies of Greek mythology. In 1954 Jung wrote, "...in Greek mythology matriarchal and patriarchal elements are about equally mixed."[5] This is an accurate statement only if one specifies that pre-Hellenic mythology is matriarchal and classical mythology is largely patriarchal. We have seen that the nature of the deities in each of these traditions varies so markedly that it is misleading to speak simply of *the* Greek myths. When Jungian psychologists purport to cite from mythology original "revelations" of the female psyche and then go back only as far as the patriarchal, revisionist portraits of the Goddesses, they are looking in the wrong place.

In addition to the character traits and deeds of the pre-Hellenic Goddesses, their symbols were radically transformed. To gloss over this transformation is to present misinformation. In a discussion of the mother archetype in mythology, Jung wrote, "Evil symbols are the witch, the dragon (or any devouring or entwining animal, such as a large fish or serpent)...This list is not, of course, complete; it presents only the most important features of the mother archetype."[6] Does it? Or does it present only features of the *patriarchal* archetype of the mother? Witches, serpents, and dragons were never "evil symbols" in the traditon of the Goddess.

When Jung spoke of archetypes and their symbols, he was reaching for "collective unconscious contents... primordial types, that is, with universal images that have existed since the remotest times."[7] In view of patriarchy's "managing of information" for the past 3500 years, their traditions of mythology and religion do not allow us full views of our earliest archetypal images. Therefore, it would seem more accurate to speak of "patriarchal archetypes," rather than "archetypes," when discussing psychological developments in patriarchal cultures such as our own.

The concept of elucidating the nature of the modern

female psyche by drawing on expressions of the female in myth is a creative and potentially profound approach. Dozens of books and scores of articles have been written by Jungians who seek such answers in Greek mythology. Unfortunately, almost none of them conveys an understanding of the two radically different systems therein. Nearly always they turn to the classical myths, composed in seventh century B.C. and even later. These are a very limited source of data on the female psyche; they are clearly tales with a point of view.

Somewhere near the beginning of Jungian treatises on this topic is usually a disclaimer about interest in any historical or social framework of the mythology: The myths are studied purely for their expressions of the unconscious. However, continual references are made to the antiquity of the myths, so as to place them far back in history. The problem is that this is almost never done specifically. For example, throughout *Women's Mysteries*, Esther Harding refers to "the ancients."[8] Does this mean our ancestors from the Neolithic, matrifocal period of culture — or the later patriarchal stage? The adjective *antique* is equally nebulous. Maria-Louise von Franz refers simply to "the antique mother-goddesses."[9] Does she mean the wise, powerful, autonomous Goddesses of the pre-Olympian era — or the petty, jealous, victimized Goddesses of the classical era? Like most of her colleagues, she would have it both ways: She states, "...the mother-goddesses depict absolutely unreflecting femininity," which is exemplified by "a terrible scene" about jealousy, for instance. Then von Franz observes "the mother-goddess always behaved like that."[10] In patriarchal mythology, that is! The Goddesses are portrayed so differently in the two traditions that there is almost nothing that "always" applies in both their pre-Hellenic and their classical versions.

Another problem is that the Great Goddess may be too large a concept for the Jungian constructs of "the feminine." Jungian analysts speak of the Goddess as being synonymous with "the feminine principle, Eros"[11] or with "feminine nature."[12] True, the Goddess was the ultimate expression of female being, but her nature was all-encompassing, e.g., giver of divine law, fierce protector, gentle nurturer. If she were a pure expression of the Jungian notion of "the feminine consciousness," these traits would not be possible. They would have to be explained via "animus energies," which would be impossible in an embodiment of pure "femininity." The Great Goddess was supreme power and was all. (For a discussion of the patriarchal biases involved in the Jungian theory of anima/animus, see *Changing of the Gods* by Naomi Goldenberg.)

An exception to most Jungian treatments of Greek Goddess mythology is "Hera: Bound and Unbound" by Murray Stein.[13] Drawing on the work of classicists, principally Kerenyi, Stein does acknowledge the difference between the pre-Hellenic and the Olympian portrayals of Hera. However, he asserts that her classical role as the archetypal wife had also been her pre-Hellenic role and that "'wifehood' was her essential mode of being."[14] Stein maintains that Hera's central goal was always "perfection in marriage."[15] This is quite impossible. Hera was a very ancient pre-Hellenic deity who was probably worshipped long before the relatively late discovery of paternity and certainly long before the invention of patriarchal marriage. She had always been associated with mating and fecundity, but this is quite different from formalized marriage. As Elizabeth Fisher pointed out in *Woman's Creation*, human history's first and longest reigning social unit was the mother and child, not the husband and wife.

A more typical example of Jungian treatments of Greek mythology as being revelatory of the modern female psyche is Robert A. Johnson's popular *She: Understanding Feminine Psychology*, subtitled *An Interpretation Based on the Myth of Amor and Psyche and Using Jungian Psychological Concepts*. Johnson opens by explaining, "the story of Amor and Psyche is one of the best elucidations available of the psychology of the feminine personality. It is an ancient, pre-Christian myth, first recorded in classical Greek times, having enjoyed a long oral tradition before that..."[16] Not *very* long. The tale of Amor and Psyche became part of the

Latin novel *The Golden Ass*, which was written in the second century A.D. by Apuleius. No doubt it was told before then, but its patriarchal aspects date the myth firmly in the classical era. Johnson further explains that "when we want to study the basic patterns of human behavior and personality, it is instructive to go to the earliest sources."[17] Absolutely right. But patriarchal myths are not they.

A principal theme of Johnson's exegesis is that every woman naturally contains "the Aphrodite nature" within her. This sounds quite plausible; after all Aphrodite was the powerful procreative energy that ensured the survival of the race. However, this original nature of Aphrodite is not what Johnson has in mind. Rather, he paints an ultra-patriarchal picture of Aphrodite that almost outdoes Apuleius: She is called "primitive femininity," with "her chief characteristics being vanity, conniving, lust, fertility, and tyranny when she is crossed."[18] (Some might find Johnson's inclusion of "fertility" among a string of negative adjectives to be clinically interesting.) In case readers may have missed the point, Johnson then labels Aphrodite "a thorough bitch" and illustrates her existence in modern females with several examples that are pregnant with woman-hating.[19] But the mental health of one individual author is not the issue. The central question raised by this approach is *What is the effect of telling a woman that much of her true nature is that of "a thorough bitch" — and that this is "proved" by "the earliest sources" of mythology?*

More than any other Jungian writer, Erich Neumann recognized the powerful implications of the long era of matrifocal mythology. He did so, however, within the boundaries of Jungian theory and so viewed "matriarchal consciousness" as an immature stage "in which the independence of the ego system is not yet fully developed."[20] Having spent years compiling the matrifocal research that became *The Great Mother,* Neumann brought to his interpretation of Amor and Psyche a comprehension of the matrifocal fragments that had survived into the patriarchal myth. Whereas Johnson sees Psyche's sisters only as "the serpent in her paradise" (an ironic metaphor on his part, to be sure) and as evil forces who are intensely jealous and who "devise a venomous plan,"[21] Neumann recognizes them as messengers of matrifocal consciousness. Their agitations correspond to a current in Psyche of "matriarchal protest" whereby she begins to question the "unconsciousness of her situation" with Eros (Amor) and her "seemingly total abandonment of her individual consciousness."[22] Neumann concludes that it is the conflict between matriarchal and patriarchal psychology that makes the myth of Amor and Psyche intelligible.[23]

As the search continues for an understanding of archetypal images, Jung would probably have us remember that an archetype is "a hypothetical model,

something like the 'pattern of behavior' in biology."²⁴
The portraits of the Goddesses in patriarchal mythology are, indeed, patterns of behavior: They are stories
told by men of how women react under patriarchy.
As such, they are two steps removed from being natural
expressions of the female mode of being. Even when
women go back to matriarchal mythology to search for
valid expressions, these are not easily captured. Their
implications nearly overwhelm us. We dance deftly
around their power. And we remember Jung's warning
about attempting to fully explain and interpret myths
and archetypes: *"The most we can do is to dream the myth
onwards and give it a modern dress."*²⁵

Mythology as a Path in the Spiritual Quest

Today we are experiencing and creating a spiritual
awakening. Many people are exploring "new" paths of
inner growth; the Judeo-Christian myths and symbols
no longer resonate for some of us, if they ever did.
Freud believed that the Judeo-Christian tradition
"keeps people stupid" because it hands them everything
and denies, even forbids, them the individual quest that
results in true growth and wisdom. Jung agreed but insisted, "Only religion can replace religion," and encouraged his patients to seek their own means of spiritual
exploration and integration. The prepatriarchal

Goddess tradition is a rich source from which women and men may draw. Yahweh/God the Father is not the omnipotent deity of all humankind, but is merely a figure in one of the many mythological/religious systems from which people may select personally meaningful aspects. In a world where spiritual expressions are valued for nurturing integration, growth, and a sense of our embeddedness in nature — rather than for providing lockstep control over a populace — diversity and evolutionary *process* are honored. Such are the values of pre- and postpatriarchal spirituality.

Since the first edition of this book appeared in 1978, the reactions have been most gratifying. A radio station in Los Angeles, for instance, reported that an interview/reading elicited more listener response than any single feature they had ever aired. Many readers have kindly written to say that the myths moved them deeply. In additon, it has been heartening to learn that artists are working in various media (e.g., theater, poetry, graphics) to extend the knowledge of our pre-Hellenic heritage beyond the closed circles of classicists. The goal of such work is not the reinstatement of prehistoric cultural structures, but rather the transmission of *possibilities*.

MYTHS

Pronunciation Guide

Gaia: Gī́-à

Pandora: Păn-dṓr-à

Themis: Thĕ́m-ĭs

Aphrodite: Ăph-rō-dī́-tē

Artemis: Ắr-tĕ-mĭs

Selene: Sĕ-lé-nē

Hecate: Hĕ́c-à-tē

Hera: Hé-rà

Athena: À-thé-nà

Demeter: Dĕ-mé-tēr

Persephone: Pēr-sĕ́ph-ō-nē

Gaia

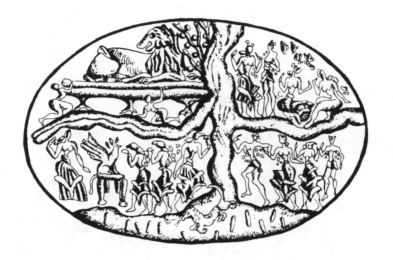

Gaia (also called Ge) is the ancient Earth-Mother who brought forth the world and the human race from "the gaping void, Chaos."[1] In the Greek imagination the earth is the abode of the dead, so the earth deity has power over the ghostly world. Because dreams, which often were felt to foreshadow the future, were believed to ascend from the netherworld, Gaia acquired an oracular function. One means of divination was incubation, in which the consultant slept in a holy shrine with her/his ear upon the ground. Another means was the pronouncements of a priestess who spoke of the future while in a trance; she sat on a tripod over vapors arising from a crevice. Gaia's oracular function appears in records of her worship at Delphi, Athens, and Aegae.[2] She was the earliest possessor of the Delphic oracle, before Poseidon, Dionysos, or Apollo.[3]

In the Homeric *Hymn to Ge*, she is praised as "the oldest of divinities"; however, the poem is clearly rooted in the Olympian tradition because it addresses Gaia as "Mother of the gods" and "wife of starry Heaven." Long before she was regarded as mother of the powerful deities, she herself was the powerful deity. In time her son/lover, Ouranos, was added to her mythology.

Although eclipsed during the classical period by the Olympian Gods, Gaia's impressive figure is always in the background. Greek citizens swore their public oaths to her.[4] The priestesses at the oracular shrine of Dodana preserved her name in their chanted litany: "Earth sends up fruits, so we praise Earth the Mother."[5] And at Delphi the priestess began her formal ritual address to the Gods thus: "First in my prayer before all other gods, I call on Earth, primeval prophetess."[6]

The Myth of Gaia

*F*REE OF BIRTH *or destruction, of time or space, of
form or condition, is the Void. From the eternal Void,
Gaia danced forth and rolled Herself into a spinning ball.
She molded mountains along Her spine, valleys in the
hollows of Her flesh. A rhythm of hills and stretching plains
followed Her contours. From Her warm moisture She bore
a flow of gentle rain that fed Her surface and brought life.
Wriggling creatures spawned in tidal pools, while tiny
green shoots pushed upward through Her pores. She filled
oceans and ponds and set rivers flowing through deep fur-
rows. Gaia watched Her plants and animals grow. In time
She brought forth from Her womb six women and six men.*

The mortals thrived but they were continually

concerned with the future. At first Gaia felt this was an amusing eccentricity on their part. However, when She saw that their worry about the future nearly consumed some of Her children, She installed among them an oracle. In the hills at the place they called Delphi, Gaia sent up steaming vapors from Her netherworld. They wafted up from a cleft in the rocks, surrounding a priestess. Gaia instructed Her priestess in the ways of entering a trance and in the interpretation of messages that arose from the darkness of Her earth-womb. The mortals travelled long distances to consult the oracle: Will my child's birth be auspicious? Will our harvest be bountiful? Will the hunt yield enough game? Will my mother survive her illness? Gaia was so moved by their stream of anxieties that She sent forth other portents of the future at Athens and Aegae.

Unceasingly the Earth-Mother manifested gifts on

Her surface and accepted the dead into Her body. In return She was revered by all mortals. Offerings to Gaia of honey and barley cake were left in a small hole in the earth before plants were gathered. Many of Her temples were built near deep chasms where yearly the mortals offered sweet cakes into Her womb. From within the darkness of Her secrets, Gaia received their gifts.

Pandora

The *kore*, or maiden, form of the Earth-Goddess is Pandora. She is pictured on ancient vessels as a figure rising from the earth with outstretched arms. (This is the often-portrayed *anodos*, the arising of the Goddess.) Sometimes she is labelled *Ge*, or *Anesidora* (she who sends up gifts), or *Pandora* (giver of all gifts).[7]

Classicists familiar with the original role of Pandora have called Hesiod's famous story, which features the Goddess as a curious, troublesome girl, a "perverted version."[8] No longer does Pandora bring the abundance of the Earth-Goddess' gifts in her great jar (*pithos*), but only disease, misery, and death.

In addition to her deed, the nature of her birth also was altered by the Olympian system of mythology. Perhaps the most spirited exposé of this transformation was written by Professor Jane Ellen Harrison in 1903: "Pandora is in ritual and matriarchal theology the earth as Kore, but in the patriarchal mythology of Hesiod her great figure is strangely changed and minished. She is no longer Earthborn, but the creature, the handiwork of Olympian Zeus... Hesiod loves the story of the Making of Pandora: he has shaped it to his own *bourgeois*, pessimistic ends; he tells it twice. Once in the *Theogany*, and here the new-born maiden has no name, she is just a 'beautiful evil,' a 'crafty snare' to mortals. But in the *Works and Days* he dares to name her and yet with infinite skill to wrest her glory into shame. Through all the magic of a poet, caught and enchanted himself by the vision of a lovely woman, there gleams the ugly malice of theological animus. Zeus the Father will have no great Earth-goddess, Mother and Maid in one, in his man-fashioned Olympus, but her figure *is* from the beginning, so he remakes it; woman, who was the inspirer, becomes the temptress; she who made all things, gods and mortals alike, is become their plaything, their slave, dowered only with physical beauty, and with a slave's tricks and blandishments. To Zeus, the arch-patriarchal *bourgeois*, the birth of the first woman is but a huge Olympian jest."[9]

The Myth of Pandora

*E*ARTH-MOTHER HAD GIVEN *the mortals
life. This puzzled them greatly. They would stare
curiously at one another, then turn away to forage for food.
Slowly they found that hunger has many forms.*

*One morning the humans followed an unusually
plump bear cub to a hillside covered with bushes that hung
heavy with red berries. They began to feast at once, hardly
aware of the tremors beginning beneath their feet. As the
quaking increased, a chasm gaped at the crest of the hill.
From it arose Pandora with Her earthen* pithos. *The mortals
were paralyzed with fear but the Goddess drew them into
Her aura.*

I am Pandora, Giver of All Gifts. *She lifted the lid*

from the large jar. From it She took a pomegranate, which became an apple, which became a lemon, which became a pear. I bring you flowering trees that bear fruit, gnarled trees hung with olives and, this, the grapevine that will sustain you. *She reached into the jar for a handful of seeds and sprinkled them over the hillside.* I bring you plants for hunger and illness, for weaving and dyeing. Hidden beneath My surface you will find minerals, ore, and clay of endless form. *She took from the jar two flat stones.* Attend with care My plainest gift: I bring you flint.

Then Pandora turned the jar on its side, inundating the hillside with Her flowing grace. The mortals were bathed in the changing colors of Her aura. I bring you wonder, curiosity, memory. I bring you wisdom. I bring you justice with mercy. I bring you caring and communal bonds. I bring you courage, strength, endurance. I bring you loving kindness for all beings. I bring you the seeds of peace.

Themis

Another of the Earth-Mother's emanations is Themis. Aeschylus portrays her as the oracular power of the earth deity and identifies her as "Themis and Gaia, one in form with many names."[10]

Themis is the force that binds people together. She is the collective conscience, the social imperative, the social order.[11] At first she is of the tribe; later in the *polis* she takes the shape of law.[12] Her name is believed to mean "steadfast," and she became the personification of justice and righteousness.[13]

In the Olympian systems, Themis is allowed two functions, though "Homer has but dim consciousness of their significance."[14] She convenes and dissolves the agora on Mount Olympus. Zeus cannot summon his own assembly; he must "bid Themis call the gods to council."[15] She also presides over feasts. When Hera arrives, the Gods rise up to greet her and hold out their cups in welcome; she takes the cup of Themis, who is first.[16]

The Myth of Themis

WHEN THE FIRST man entered a cave and witnessed the first woman's magic of drawing forth a new person from her body, Themis was there. The young shall be fed and nurtured, protected and loved. *The humans increased in number, living together in small groups. They shared meat, nuts, plants, shelter, and the pleasure of their bodies. Themis was with them.* All who shared the bond of a woman's womb, you are her Family. You are indivisible. *The families multiplied, each woman giving birth within the aura of her mother's protection. Themis saw their needs.* All the families descended from one womb are a clan. Stay together. Listen to the elders as I guide them. *Neighboring clans sought better water sources, needed new shelters, settled common ground. Themis united them in peace.* You who pass birth, love, and death on shared ground, who trade your skills and crops among your clans, you are a Village. Follow the judgments of your council as I guide them. *The villages spread into towns, sometimes cities. Themis watched and issued from Her oracles pronouncements of order, justice, and mercy.* Keep central your agora. There I will reveal the Law to your leaders. Swear your oaths in My name and they will stand until you are received into My earth-womb. Grow in righteousness. I will feed you.

In this way, millennia passed and Greece prospered in her infancy. Innocence ended abruptly. Barbarian invaders swept down through her mainland and later her islands. They seized Themis at the outset. With the Goddess a bound captive, the invaders proclaimed the new order:

Children must be named after their fathers; cities must be fortified; power must be worshipped. They established their new god, Zeus, who ruled by the terror of his thunderbolt and procreated by deception and rape. Yet Themis would not be silenced. You dare not crush the primal Order. When your new gods and your mutilations of our old Goddesses assemble on Mount Olympus, I alone will have the right to convoke them. I will not die.

Aphrodite

Aphrodite is a fertility Goddess, the primal mother of all on-going creation.[17] She is a virgin in the original sense (one-in-herself, not necessarily abstaining from sex but always remaining independent),[18] and has eternal beauty. Her sea birth is yet another version (along with that of Pandora and Persephone) of the *anodos*, the arising of the Goddess.[19] Her ritual bath of renewal at Paphos is associated with that of Hera and Athena.[20]

In Crete the epithet *Antheia* (flower goddess) was connected with Aphrodite at Knossos. The title reveals an old link with herbal magic, and she is associated with the apple myrtle, poppy, rose, and water-mint.[21] She is also maker of the morning dew.[22]

Aphrodite came into Greece through Cyprus and originally was from western Asia, where a young lover, Adonis, eventually was added to her mythology. The Goddess was akin especially to Ishtar and Astarte.[23] In name, personality, and function she was unHellenic and, in contrast to Athena, she was not really Hellenized by the time the Homeric poems were written. There she is "thoroughly anti-Achaean and treated with little respect."[24] Professor Harrison once again has strong words about the transformation of the Goddess: "When Aphrodite is assimilated into the patriarchal Olympus, a foolish and futile attempt is made to fit her out with a husband: the craftsman, Hephaistos."[25] The net in which Homer represents Aphrodite as being caught by Hephaestus was originally her own as Goddess of the Sea, and her priestess seems to have worn it during the spring festival.[26]

Patriarchal tradition revised the story of the birth of Aphrodite to a rather extreme extent: This powerful, procreative Goddess from Asia is portrayed as having been produced by the sea foam caused by the severed genitals of Ouranos, who had been castrated by his son, Cronos.

The Myth of Aphrodite

*L*IFE WAS YOUNG *and frail when Aphrodite arose with the breath of renewal. Born by gentle winds on the eastern sea, She alighted on the island of Cyprus. So graceful and alluring was the Goddess that the Seasons rushed to meet Her, imploring Her always to stay. Aphrodite smiled. Her stay would be never ending, Her work never complete. She crossed the pebbled beach and wandered over the hills and plains, seeking out all living creatures. Magically She touched them with desire and sent them off in joyous pairs. She blessed the females' wombs, guarded them as they grew, and warded off love's pains at birth. Everywhere Aphrodite drew forth the hidden promise of life. Every day She kissed the earth with morning dew.*

The wanderings of the Goddess carried Her far, yet each spring She returned with Her doves to Cyprus for Her sacred bath at Paphos. There She was attended by Her Graces: Flowering, Growth, Beauty, Joy, and Radiance. They crowned Her with myrtle and lay a path of rose petals at Her feet. Aphrodite walked into the sea, into the pulsing moon rhythms of the tide. When She emerged with Her spirit renewed, spring blossomed fully and all beings felt Her joy. Through seasons, years, eras, Aphrodite's mysteries remain inviolable, for She alone understands the love that begets life.

Triad of the Moon:
Artemis, Selene, Hecate

Artemis is the Goddess of untamed nature. Among the rustic people, she is the most popular Goddess in Greece.[27] "Where has Artemis not danced?" is a Greek saying.[28] Central to her worship are ecstatic dances and the sacred bough,[29] most probably derived from worship of the ancient moon tree, source of immortality, secret knowledge, and inspiration.[30] Artemis assists females of all species in childbirth and gave the name *artemisia* to the medicinal herb now called mugwort, which is used to encourage delivery.[31]

Although Artemis was worshipped throughout Greece, she was especially venerated in Arcadia. There she dwelt apart in wild, untouched forests and was the most virginal of all the Goddesses.[32] The other important site of her worship was at Ephesus in Anatolia, where her qualities of Mother Goddess were emphasized. The Ephesians believed that a many-breasted image of Artemis fell from heaven.[33] (Eventually this phenomenon took the form of a breastplate garment on statuary.) Two early forms of this Goddess were Britomaris of eastern Crete and Diktynna of western Crete.[34]

In Olympian mythology Artemis is made the sister of Apollo and the daughter of Zeus. Her mother is variously represented as Demeter or Persephone or, most commonly, Leto.[35] Her Arcadian nature as Lady of the Beasts is employed in her new role as patron of hunters. Early graphic representations of Artemis show her flanked by two lions or in ecstatic dance with a stag; later she is shown standing on a lion; finally she stands with her bow, holding a slain deer in each hand. In the *Iliad* Homer gives Artemis "a feeble and even ridiculous part."[36]

Selene (also called Mene) is the moon Goddess who pulls the full moon across the sky with her chariot. She usually drives oxen or steers, or sometimes horses. In her early forms, she herself is conceived of as a cow with the ancient "horns of consecration," which form a crescent moon. Selene is said to be "of great importance in magic,"[37] but little trace of her worship has survived.

Hecate is the Goddess of the waning and dark moon. She has chthonic associations and rules over ghosts and demons. Ritually prescribed food, known as "Hecate's suppers," was offered to her as a form of purification, and her image was set before homes to avert evil.[38] She is adept at sorcery and is "the mother of witches."[39] At certain sites in Greece, Hecate's torches were carried around the freshly sown fields to promote their fertility.[40]

Olympian mythology portrays Hecate as the daughter of Hera and Zeus. In one of the patriarchal stories assigned to her, Hecate enrages her mother by stealing her rouge to give to Europa. Hecate flees to the earth and hides in the house of a woman who is in labor; her contact with this woman is said to render the Goddess "impure."[41]

The Myth of the
Triad of the Moon:
Artemis, Selene, Hecate

WHEN THE MOON *appeared as a slender crescent, delicate and fine but firm in the promise of growth, Artemis roamed the untouched forests of Arcadia. The Goddess lived with Her nymphs amid the thick, wild growth where animals joined freely in Her games and dances. She loved new life. Whether at play or at rest, Artemis was ever alert for the rising moans of a mother giving birth. The wind brought to Her long, low sighs and staccato songs of pain expelled. If the mother was an animal, lying alone in a hidden cave or a sheltered pile of leaves, Artemis rushed deftly through the woods to her side. She*

*brought leaves of Her wild artemisia for the animal to eat
and spoke softly in the mother's own sounds. The Goddess
gently stroked the bulging womb until the wet, squirming
bodies emerged. She fondled each one and placed them
under Her protection:* Within these forests no harm will
touch the children of Artemis.

*If the mother was a human, the Goddess appeared
instantly at her side bringing artemisia for a potent tea.
She wiped the woman's brow and massaged her womb with
delicacy and patience, even though She knew the result
would be only a meager litter of one or sometimes two. Still,
Artemis always appeared to a mother who called and
always rejoiced with her at the moment of birth. The other
mortals present would come forward for a look, asking,
"How is the new one? Who is the new one?" Then Artemis
would smile at the new One and whisper to the mother:* You

may both enter My forests without fear and join Me on any night lit by the waxing moon.

The joining began when the moon was new and continued each night with more and more of Her animals and humans coming to dance with Artemis. On the evening before the full moon Her sacred grove was filled with cele-brants. They encircled a large tree that stood apart from the others, its smooth bark and leaves seeming silver in the moon-light. Artemis moved toward the tree and silence followed, but for Her doves cooing softly in the boughs overhead. The Goddess crouched as the Great She-Bear She once had been and touched the earth. From the roots, up the trunk, along the branches to the leaves She drew her hands. Again. And Again. With each pass She brought forth new life: pale blossoms unfolding and falling away, tiny globes of fruit shining among the branches, and finally ripe, glowing fruit hanging from the sacred boughs. Artemis gathered the fruit and fed Her animals, Her mortals, Her nymphs, and Herself. The dance began.

The animals were drawn to the tree. They rolled over its roots and encircled the trunk. In a larger ring the dancers raised their arms, turning slowly, and felt currents of energy rising through their trunks, turning faster, through their arms, turning, out their fingers, turning, turning, to their heads, whirling, racing, flying. Sparks of energy flew from their fingertips, lacing the air with traces of clear blue light. They joined hands, joined arms, merged bodies into a circle of unbroken current that carried them effortlessly. Artemis appeared large before them standing straight against the tree, Her spine its trunk, Her arms its boughs. Her body pulsed with life, its rhythms echoed by the silvered tree, the animals at Her feet, the dancers, the grass, the plants, the grove. Every particle of the forest quivered with Her energy. Artemis the nurturer, protector, Goddess of the swelling moon. Artemis! She began to merge with the sacred tree, while the circle of dancers spun around Her. They threw back their heads and saw the shimmering boughs rush by. When Artemis was one with the moon tree, the circle broke. Dancers went whirling through the grove, falling exhausted on the mossy forest floor.

Lying there on the earth, still breathing in rhythm with the earth, they stared up at the constant dancers in the heavens. Through the stars Selene was cutting a path with Her chariot. The winged Goddess drove a pair of oxen, whose horns echoed the crescent moon on Her own crown. Behind Her Selene pulled the full moon across the sky. She rose from the ocean and climbed steadily with the enormous disc to Her zenith, where it gradually shrank in size and She easily glided downward to the ocean once again. When Selene crossed the heavens, Her light flooded the earth, filtering down through the hidden cracks and crevices in the nature of mortal beings. They marked Her passage, joined in small groups to celebrate, and treated with awe those touched by Her magic.

But when the moon slipped away, shrinking gracefully into its own death, there were no festivities. The nights grew blacker and the mortals guarded themselves against visiting spirits from the underworld. Hoards of ghosts led by Hecate and Her baying hounds roamed the earth on moonless nights. Yet She protected those mortals who purified themselves in Her name. With faces averted they offered Her ritual suppers at lonely crossroads, the gathering place of spirits. When Hecate's rites were observed, the black nights passed silently one into another. But if the

Goddess was defied, She unleashed the power of Her wrath and swept over the earth, bringing storms and destruction. Animals howled in fright, while Her ghosts stalked freely.

Hecate's disturbances were fierce, yet not all of the mortals feared them. Some longed to join Her. In the dark of the moon small covens awaited Her near drooping willow trees. She appeared suddenly before them with Her torch and Her hounds. A nest of snakes writhed in Her hair, sometimes shedding, sometimes renewing. Until the new moon slit the sky, Hecate shared clues to Her secrets. Those who believed understood. They saw that form was not fixed, watched human become animal become tree become human. They witnessed the power of Her favored herbs: black poppy, smilax, mandragora, aconite. Awesome were Her skills but always Hecate taught the same lesson: Without death there is no life.

Hera

Hera is essentially the Goddess of women and fecundity.[42] Her connection with the three seasons of antiquity corresponds to the three stages of woman's life (maiden, fertile woman, elder).[43] In addition, she is connected to the three stages of the moon; such was the harmony with nature in earlier times that women's periodicity followed the moon's phases closely and their menstruation began at the new moon,[44] which was often summoned by their choruses.[45]

Hera was venerated at many sites in Greece, particularly on Crete and on Samos, but the chief center of her worship was at Argos. There several shrines were built to her, and she returned every year for a ritual bath in the spring Kanathos to renew her sense of virginity.[46] She also presided over "the sacred marriage," the merging of the lunar cow and the solar bull, which was a celebration of renewal and fertility in nature, especially that of the soil.[47] On Samos the sanctuary built for Hera was never exceeded in size by any temple in Greece.[48] The Samian women used *lygos* branches to stimulate menstruation and to aid in purification during their days of abstinence at the feast of the Thesmophoria[49] (see notes preceding the myth of Demeter and Persephone). (In order to present an inclusive portrait of Hera, the Argive and Samian forms of worship are combined in the following myth.)

At Olympia the Goddess' Heraion long predates the temple of Zeus.[50] There races were run among the women "from time immemorial."[51] The runners were selected from three age groups, representing the three phases of the moon. "The well-founded view" among classicists is that the girls' races, which were held every four years at the feast of the Heraia, were far more ancient than the boys' races, which were first introduced only in the seventh century B.C.[52] When the men built a stadium at Olympia, an altar to Hera was included to commemorate her earlier reign. However, the only woman allowed to watch the contests was the priestess of Demeter Chamaine, the Goddess linked with the soil, "probably because the competing men were later arrivals and had taken the ground for the stadium away from Demeter."[53]

In patriarchal mythology Hera becomes the wife of Zeus, although the connection of Zeus with Hera is a "late and superficial usage."[54] Hera is portrayed as Zeus' troublesome, disagreeable wife in a stormy marriage. The archaic theme of parthenogenesis is found in Homer's work several times in connection with Hera, linking her to the older matrifocal world.[55]

Professor Harrison summarizes the fate of the Goddess: "Hera was indigenous and represents a matrilinear system; she reigned alone at Argos, at Samos; her temple at Olympia is distinct from and far earlier than that of Zeus. Her first husband, or rather consort, was Herakles. The conquering Northerners pass from Dodona to Thessaly. Zeus drops his real shadow-wife,

Dione, at Dodona in passing from Thessaly to Olympia, and at Olympia, after the fashion of a conquering chieftain, marries Hera, a daughter of the land. In Olympos Hera seems merely the jealous and quarrelsome wife. In reality she reflects the turbulent native princess, coerced but never really subdued by an alien conqueror."[56]

The Myth of Hera

O N THE MORNING of the new moon, the women of Argos left their homes and walked together to the Stream of the Freeing Water. They bathed and then gathered branches from the nearby lygos bushes, which they laid in a large circular bower. On this ring they sat throughout the day, each seated with the women of her mother's clan. With the blessing of the Goddess, the lygos encouraged the flow of their sacred blood that would complete the cleansing they had begun in the stream. Although the women fasted, their mood was not somber. They talked of their crops, their herds, their children and listened to stories told by the elders. As twilight approached, they began chants and songs that summoned Hera, in Her manifestation of the new moon. When Hera appeared as a pale sliver climbing above the horizon, the women responded by lighting a fire in the center of their circle and continued the songs. Gradually Hera drew forth the blood of purification and renewed fertility. Those who received Her gift were honored. All rose, giving praise to the Goddess, and returned in a torchlit procession to their homes.

Hidden in the foothills nearby, the spring called Kanathos flowed secretly, silently from Earth's womb. Each year Hera appeared to the Argive women at the spring. She bathed in the cool water and emerged with Her virginity renewed once again—One-In-Herself, the Celestial Virgin. The women received the blessing of Hera's grace and crowned one another with wreaths of aster, blossoming with the Goddess' starflowers. They followed Hera to a broad terrace on the side of Mount Euboia, Her sacred ground.

The Goddess looked down onto the plain stretching out before Her. All the people of Argos, all the animals, all the colors of spring had come together for the Sacred Marriage. Hera presided over the merging of the lunar cow and the solar bull. Then She looked out over the assembly and blessed the Argives with unfailing fecundity of field and womb. They celebrated the promise of their survival with dances and feasting. On that day began again the homage to Hera which continued throughout the year.

Every four years the benevolence of the Goddess was celebrated at the feast of the Heraia. At Olympia Hera watched the footraces run in Her name. The races were run by girls divided into three age groups to represent the three phases of the moon and the corresponding three stages of woman's life. The winners were awarded an olive wreath and the honor of resembling the Goddess most *closely. As Hera crowned the youngest winner, the girl addressed the crowd:* I am the new moon, swelling with magic, pure in my maidenhood, ever growing stronger. *The second winner spoke:* I am the full moon, complete in my powers, making people with my rhythms, bathing them in light. *The third said:* I am the waning moon, easing into peace, knowing all that went before, I am the wise one.

Athena

Athena (or Athene) was originally a Cretan Goddess who watched over the home and town. Attributes of fertility and renewal are expressed in her association with tree (or pillar) and snake symbolism, respectively.[57] She is patron of wisdom, arts, and skills, and she especially protects architects, sculptors, potters, spinners, and weavers.[58] Athena was also the Goddess of the matrifocal Pelasgoi of the Peloponnese;[59] in addition to her strong following on Crete, she was venerated at the following pre-Hellenic sites: Argos, Sparta, Troy, Smyrna, Epidaurus, Troezen, and Pheneus.[60]

When the Mycenaean princes of the mainland adopted and adapted Athena, she was assigned a martial character.[61] She became the shielded defender of their citadels, particularly Athens.

In Olympian mythology Athena is firmly established as the cold, rigid Goddess of war. So suppressed and/or forgotten are her matrifocal Cretan origins that she is represented as a daughter born without a mother, having sprung fully armed from the head of Zeus.

The Myth of Athena

I N THE MINOAN DAYS of Crete an unprecedented flowering of learning and the arts was cultivated by Athena. Dynamic architecture rose to four stories, pillared and finely detailed, yet always infused with the serenity of the Goddess. Patiently Her mortals charted the heavens, devised a calendar, kept written archives. In the palaces they painted striking frescoes of Her priestesses and sculpted Her owl and ever-renewing serpent in the shrine rooms. Goddess figures and their rituals were deftly engraved on seals and amulets. Graceful scenes were cast in relief for gold vessels and jewelry. Athena nurtured all the arts, but Her favorites were weaving and pottery.

Long before there were palaces, the Goddess had

appeared to a group of women gathering plants in a field. She broke open the stems of blue-flowered flax and showed them how the threadlike fibers could be spun and then woven. The woof and warp danced in Her fingers until a length of cloth was born before them. She told them which plants and roots would color the cloth, and then She led the mortals from the field to a pit of clay. There they watched Athena form a long serpent and coil it, much like the serpents coiled around Her arms. She formed a vessel and smoothed the sides, then deftly applied a paste made from another clay and water. When it was baked in a hollow in the earth, a spiral pattern emerged clearly. The image of circles that repeat and repeat yet move forward was kept by the women for centuries.

As the mortals moved forward, Athena guided the impulse of the arts. She knew they would never flourish in an air of strife, so She protected households from divisive forces and guarded towns against aggression. So invincible was the aura of Her protection that the Minoans lived in unfortified coastal towns. Their shipping trade prospered, and they enjoyed a peace that spanned a thousand years. To Athena each family held the olive bough sacred, each worshipped Her in their home. Then quite suddenly the flowering of the Minoans was slashed. Northern barbarians, more fierce than the Aegean Goddess had ever known, invaded the island and carried Athena away to Attica. There they made Her a soldier.

Demeter and
Persephone

Demeter is the Grain-Mother, the giver of crops. Her origins are Cretan, and she has been strongly connected to Gaia[62] and to Isis.[63] Demeter's daughter, Persephone, or Kore, is the Grain-Maiden, who embodies the new crop. Every autumn the women of early Greece observed a three-day, agricultural fertility ritual, the Thesmophoria, in honor of Demeter. The three days were called the *Kathodos* and *Anodos* (Downgoing and Uprising), the *Nesteia* (Fasting), and the *Kalligeneia* (Fair-Born or Fair Birth).[64] The Thesmophoria, the Arrephoria, the Skirophoria, the Stenia, and the Haloa were rites practiced by women only and were of extremely early origin. They were preserved "in pristine purity down to the late days and were left almost uncontaminated by Olympian usage"; they emerged later in the most widely influential of all Greek rituals, the Eleusinian Mysteries.[65] Isocrates wrote that Demeter brought to Attica "twofold gifts": "crops" and the "Rite of Initiation"; "those who partake of the rite have fairer hopes concerning the end of life."[66]

The Homeric *Hymn to Demeter*, assigned to the seventh century B.C., is a story written to explain the Eleusinian Mysteries, which honored Demeter.[67] The tale became famous as "The Rape of Persephone," who was carried off to the underworld and forced to become the bride of Hades. However, prior to the Olympian version of the myth at a rather late date, there was no mention of rape in the ancient cult of

Demeter and her daughter, nor was there any rape in the two traditions antecedent to Demeter's mythology.

Archaeology has supported[68] what Diodorus wrote concerning the flow of Egyptian culture into Greece via Crete: "the whole mythology of Hades" was brought from Egypt into Greece and the mysteries of Isis are just like those of Demeter, "the names only being changed."[69] Isis was Queen of the Underworld, sister of Osiris, and passed freely to and from the netherworld. Demeter's other antecedent was Gaia,[70] the ancient Earth-Mother who had power over the underworld because the earth is the abode of the dead.[71] At certain sites in Greece, Demeter was worshipped as "Demeter Chthonia,"[72] and in Athens the dead were called *Demetreioi*, "Demeter's People"; not only did she bring all things to life, but when they died, she received them back into her bosom.[73] That the maiden form (Kore) of the Goddess would share the functions of the mature form (Demeter), as giver of crops on the earth and ruler of the underworld, is a natural extension. The early Greeks often conceived of their Goddesses in maiden and mature form simultaneously; later the maiden was called "daughter."[74]

In addition to the connections with Isis and Gaia, another theory holds that Persephone (also called Phesephatta) was a very old Goddess of the underworld indigenous to Attica, who was assimilated by the first wave of invaders from the north; the myth of the abduction is believed to be an artificial link that merged Persephone with Demeter's daughter, Kore.[75] Whatever the impulse behind portraying Persephone as a rape victim, evidence indicates that this twist to the story was added after the societal shift from matrifocal to patriarchal, and that it was not part of the original mythology. In fact, it is likely that the story of the rape of the Goddess is a historical reference to the invasion of the northern Zeus-worshippers, just as is the story of the stormy marriage of Hera, the native queen who will not yield to the conqueror Zeus.

Although the exact delineation of the pre-Olympian version of the myth of Demeter and Persephone has been lost, the following version seeks to approximate the original by employing the surviving clues and evidence. This extremely ancient and widely revered sacred story of mother and daughter long pre-dates the Judeo-Christian deification of father and son.

The Myth of
Demeter and Persephone

T HERE ONCE WAS no winter. Leaves and vines,
flowers and grass grew into fullness and faded into
decay, then began again in unceasing rhythms.

Men joined with other men of their mother's clan
and foraged in the evergreen woods for game. Women
with their children or grandchildren toddling behind ex-
plored the thick growth of plants encircling their homes.
They learned eventually which bore fruits that sated hunger,
which bore leaves and roots that chased illness and pain,
and which worked magic on the eye, mouth, and head.

The Goddess Demeter watched fondly as the mortals
learned more and more about Her plants. Seeing that their

lives were difficult and their food supply sporadic, She was moved to give them the gift of wheat. She showed them how to plant the seed, cultivate, and finally harvest the wheat and grind it. Always the mortals entrusted the essential process of planting food to the women, in the hope that their fecundity of womb might be transferred to the fields they touched.

Demeter had a fair-born Daughter, Persephone, who watched over the crops with Her Mother. Persephone was drawn especially to the new sprouts of wheat that pushed their way through the soil in Her favorite shade of tender green. She loved to walk among the young plants, beckoning them upward and stroking the weaker shoots.

Later, when the plants approached maturity, Persephone would leave their care to Her Mother and wander over the hills, gathering narcissus, hyacinth, and garlands of myrtle for Demeter's hair. Persephone Herself favored the bold red poppies that sprang up among the wheat. It was not unusual to see Demeter and Persephone decked with flowers dancing together through open fields and gently sloping valleys. When Demeter felt especially fine, tiny shoots of barley or oats would spring up in the footprints She left.

One day They were sitting on the slope of a high hill looking out in many directions over Demeter's fields of grain. Persephone lay on Her back while Her Mother stroked Her long hair idly.

Mother, sometimes in my wanderings I have met the spirits of the dead hovering around their earthly homes and sometimes the mortals, too, can see them in the dark of the moon by the light of their fires and torches.

There are those spirits who drift about restlessly, but they mean no harm.

I spoke to them, Mother. They seem confused and many do not even understand their own state. Is there no one in the netherworld who receives the newly dead?

Demeter sighed and answered softly, It is I who has domain over the underworld. From beneath the surface of the earth I draw forth the crops and the wild plants. And in pits beneath the surface of the earth I have instructed the mortals to store My seed from harvest until sowing, in order that contact with the spirits of My underworld will fertilize the seed. Yes, I know very well the realm of the dead, but My most important work is here. I must feed the living.

Persephone rolled over and thought about the ghostly

spirits She had seen, about their faces drawn with pain and bewilderment.

The dead need us, Mother. I will go to them.

Demeter abruptly sat upright as a chill passed through Her and rustled the grass around Them. She was speechless for a moment, but then hurriedly began recounting all the pleasures they enjoyed in Their world of sunshine, warmth, and fragrant flowers. She told Her Daughter of the dark gloom of the underworld and begged Her to reconsider.

Persephone sat up and hugged Her Mother and rocked Her with silent tears. For a long while They held each other, radiating rainbow auras of love and protection. Yet Persephone's response was unchanged.

They stood and walked in silence down the slope toward the fields. Finally They stopped, surrounded by Demeter's grain, and shared weary smiles.

Very well. You are loving and giving and We cannot give only to Ourselves. I understand why You must go. Still, You are My Daughter and for every day that You remain in the underworld, I will mourn Your absence.

Persephone gathered three poppies and three sheaves of wheat. Then Demeter led Her to a long, deep chasm and produced a torch for Her to carry. She stood and watched Her Daughter go down farther and farther into the cleft in the earth.

In the crook of Her arm Persephone held Her Mother's grain close to Her breast, while Her other arm held the torch aloft. She was startled by the chill as She descended, but She was not afraid. Deeper and deeper into the darkness She continued, picking Her way slowly along the rocky path. For many hours She was surrounded only by silence. Gradually She became aware of a low moaning

sound. It grew in intensity until She rounded a corner and

entered an enormous cavern, where thousands of spirits of

the dead milled about aimlessly, hugging themselves, shaking

their heads, and moaning in despair.

Persephone moved through the forms to a large, flat

rock and ascended. She produced a stand for Her torch, a

vase for Demeter's grain, and a large shallow bowl piled

with pomegranate seeds, the food of the dead. As She stood

before them, Her aura increased in brightness and in

warmth.

I am Persephone and I have come to be your

Queen. Each of you has left your earthly body and now

resides in the realm of the dead. If you come to Me, I

will initiate you into your new world.

She beckoned those nearest to step up onto the rock

and enter Her aura. As each spirit crossed before Her,
Persephone embraced the form and then stepped back and
gazed into the eyes. She reached for a few of the pomegranate
seeds, squeezing them between Her fingers. She painted the
forehead with a broad swatch of the red juice and slowly
pronounced:

You have waxed into the fullness of life

And waned into darkness;

May you be renewed in tranquility and wisdom.

For months Persephone received and renewed the
dead without ever resting or even growing weary. All the
while Her Mother remained disconsolate. Demeter roamed
the earth hoping to find Her Daughter emerging from one
of the secret clefts. In Her sorrow She withdrew Her power
from the crops, the trees, the plants. She forbade any new
growth to blanket the earth. The mortals planted their

seed, but the fields remained barren. Demeter was consumed with loneliness and finally settled on a bare hillside
to gaze out at nothing from sunken eyes. For days and nights,
weeks and months She sat waiting.

One morning a ring of purple crocus quietly pushed
its way through the soil and surrounded Demeter. She
looked with surprise at the new arrivals from below and
thought what a shame it was that She was too weakened
to feel rage at Her injunction being broken. Then she leaned
forward and heard them whisper in the warm breeze:
"Persephone returns! Persephone returns!"

Demeter leapt to Her feet and ran down the hill
through the fields into the forests. She waved Her arms
and cried: Persephone returns! Everywhere Her energy
was stirring, pushing, bursting forth into tender greenery
and pale young petals. Animals shed old fur and rolled in

the fresh, clean grass while birds sang out: "Persephone returns! Persephone returns!"

When Persephone ascended from a dark chasm, there was Demeter with a cape of white crocus for Her Daughter. They ran to each other and hugged and cried and laughed and hugged and danced and danced and danced. The mortals saw everywhere the miracles of Demeter's bliss and rejoiced in the new life of spring. Each winter they join Demeter in waiting through the bleak season of Her Daughter's absence. Each spring they are renewed by the signs of Persephone's return.

NOTES
BIBLIOGRAPHY

Notes

Introduction

1. Robert Graves, *The Greek Myths*, Vol. 1, Middlesex, England: Penguin Books, 1960 (1955), p. 22.

2. C. G. Jung, *Collected Works*, Vol. 9, Princeton: Princeton University Press, Bollingen Series 20, 1969 (1959), part i, par. 316.

3. *Ibid.*, par. 6.

4. *Ibid.*, par. 26.

5. Jung, *Collected Works*, Vol. 11, par. 711.

6. Jung, *Collected Works*, Vol. 9, part i, par. 157.

7. *Ibid.*, par. 316.

8. M. Esther Harding, *Women's Mysteries, Ancient and Modern*, London: Rider & Company, 1971 (1955), p. 103.

9. Marie-Louise von Franz, *The Feminine in Fairytales*, Irving, Texas: Spring Publications, 1972, p. 22.

10. *Ibid.*

11. Harding, p. 34.

12. von Franz, p. 28.

13. Murray Stein, "Hera: Bound and Unbound," *Spring*, 1977, pp. 105–119.

14. *Ibid.*, pp. 106–107.

15. *Ibid.*, p. 114.

16. Robert A. Johnson, *She: Understanding Feminine Psychology*, New York: Harper & Row, 1977, p. 1.

17. *Ibid.*

18. *Ibid.*, p. 6.

19. *Ibid.*, p. 7.

20. Erich Neumann, *The Great Mother: An Analysis of the Archetype*, Princeton: Princeton University Press, Bollingen Series 47, 1963 (1955), p. 78.

21. Johnson, pp. 18–19.

22. Erich Neumann, *Amor and Psyche: The Psychic Development of the Feminine*, Princeton: Princeton University Press, Bollingen Series 54, 1956, p. 76.

23. *Ibid.*, p. 146.

24. Jung, *Collected Works*, Vol. 9, part i, par. 5n.

25. *Ibid.*, par. 271.

Text Preceding Each Myth

1. H. J. Rose, *A Handbook of Greek Mythology*, New York: E. P. Dutton & Co., Inc., 1950, p. 19.

2. Lewis R. Farnell, *The Cults of the Greek States*, Vol. 3, Oxford: Oxford University Press, 1907, p. 8.

3. Jane Ellen Harrison, *Myths of Greece and Rome*, London: Ernest Benn Ltd., 1927, p. 68.

4. Farnell, p. 3.

5. Harrison, *Myths of Greece and Rome*, p. 68.

6. *Ibid.*

7. Jane Ellen Harrison, *Prolegomena to the Study of Greek Religion*, Cambridge: Cambridge University Press, 1922 (1903), pp. 280–281.

8. Farnell, p. 27.

9. Harrison, *Prolegomena to the Study of Greek Religion*, pp. 284–285.

10. Jane Ellen Harrison, *Themis: A Study of the Social Origins of Greek Religion*, Cambridge: Cambridge University Press, 1912, p. 480.

11. Harrison, *Themis*, pp. 485 and 533.

12. *Ibid.*, p. 484.

13. *The Oxford Classical Dictionary*, Second Edition, 1970, p. 1052.

14. Harrison, *Themis*, p. 482.

15. *Ibid.* (Homer, *Iliad*, XX. 4–6).

16. *Ibid.*

17. E. O. James, *The Cult of the Mother Goddess: An Archaeological and Documentary Study*, New York: Frederick A. Praeger, Inc., 1959, p. 147.

18. Harrison, *Myths of Greece and Rome*, p. 26; also M. Esther Harding, *Women's Mysteries, Ancient and Modern*, London: Rider & Company, 1971 (1955), p. 103.

19. Harrison, *Prolegomena to the Study of Greek Religion*, p. 309.

20. *Ibid.*, p. 311.

21. R. F. Willetts, *Cretan Cults and Festivals*, London: Routledge and Kegan Paul, 1962, p. 285.

22. *Ibid.*

23. James, p. 147.

24. *Ibid.*

25. Harrison, *Myths of Greece and Rome*, p. 26.

26. Robert Graves, *The Greek Myths*, Vol. 1, Middlesex, England: Penguin Books, 1960 (1955), p. 71.

27. Martin P. Nilsson, *The Minoan-Mycenaean Religion*, New York: Biblo and Tannen, 1971, p. 503.

28. *Ibid.*

29. Martin P. Nilsson, *A History of Greek Religion*, Oxford: Oxford University Press, 1949, p. 28; also *Ibid.*, p. 503.

30. Harding, p. 46.

31. Harrison, *Myths of Greece and Rome*, p. 37.

32. *Ibid.*, p. 33.

33. James, p. 151.

34. Nilsson, *The Minoan-Mycenaean Religion*, pp. 510–511.

35. *New Larousse Encyclopedia of Mythology*, English Edition, London: Prometheus Press, The Hamlyn Publishing Group Ltd., 1968, p. 121.

36. *The Oxford Classical Dictionary*, p. 127.

37. Rose, p. 34.

38. Nilsson, *A History of Greek Religion*, pp. 204–205; also James, p. 153.

39. Robert Graves, *The White Goddess*, New York: Farrar, Straus and Giroux, 1966, p. 200.

40. Harding, p. 129.

41. *New Larousse Encyclopedia of Mythology*, p. 165.

42. James, p. 144.

43. Harrison, *Myths of Greece and Rome*, p. 19.

44. C. Kerenyi, *Zeus and Hera*, Princeton: Princeton University Press, Bollingen Series 65-5, 1975, p. 130.

45. *Ibid.*, p. 126.

46. Harrison, *Prolegomena to the Study of Greek Religion*, p. 311.

47. James, p. 144.

48. Kerenyi, p. 149.

49. *Ibid.*, p. 155.

50. Harrison, *Myths of Greece and Rome*, p. 18; also Kerenyi, pp. 133 and 135.

51. Kerenyi, p. 133.

52. *Ibid.*, p. 134.

53. *Ibid.*, p. 133.

54. Willetts, p. 111.

55. Kerenyi, p. 56.

56. Harrison, *Themis*, p. 491.

57. James, p. 146.

58. *New Larousse Encyclopedia of Mythology*, p. 107.

59. George Thomson, *The Prehistoric Aegean*, New York: The Citadel Press, 1965 (1949), p. 267.

60. Graves, *The Greek Myths*, Vol. 1, p. 47.

61. James, p. 146; also Nilsson, *A History of Greek Religion*, pp. 26–27.

62. Farnell, pp. 28 and 48–50.

63. Harrison, *The Religion of Ancient Greece*, London: Archibald Constable & Co. Ltd., 1905, pp. 51–52.

64. Harrison, *Prolegomena to the Study of Greek Religion*, pp. 120–131; also Willetts, p. 152.

65. *Ibid.*, Harrison, p. 120.

66. Harrison, *The Religion of Ancient Greece*, p. 51.

67. James, p. 153.

68. Sir Arthur Evans, *The Earlier Religion of Greece in the Light of Cretan Discoveries*, London: Macmillan and Co. Ltd., 1931, p. 8.

69. Harrison, *The Religion of Ancient Greece*, p. 52.

70. Farnell, pp. 28 and 48–50.

71. *Ibid.*, p. 8.

72. *Ibid.*, pp. 48–50.

73. Harrison, *Myths of Greece and Rome*, p. 73.

74. Harrison, *Prolegomena to the Study of Greek Religion*, pp. 263 and 274.

75. Gunther Zuntz, *Persephone: Three Essays on Religion and Thought in Magna Graecia*, Oxford: Oxford University Press, 1971, pp. 75–77.

Bibliography

Note: This is not a complete bibliography of all the books I consulted but, rather, a listing of those that were most relevant to the pre-Hellenic Goddesses. Many would also be useful to anyone wishing to rediscover the original nature of closeted Goddesses in other cultures. — C.S.

J. J. Bachofen. *Myth, Religion, and Mother Right*, translated by Ralph Mannheim. Princeton: Princeton University Press, Bollingen Series 84, 1967 (1854).

John Boardman. *Greek Gems and Finger Rings*. New York: Harry N. Abrams, Inc., 1972.

Robert Briffault. *The Mothers*. London: George Allen & Unwin Ltd., abridged edition, 1959 (1927).

Z. Budapest. *Selene: The Most Famous Bulleaper on Earth*. Oakland: Diana Press, 1976.

Joseph Campbell. *The Masks of God: Primitive Mythology* New York: The Viking Press, 1959.
The Masks of God: Occidental Mythology. New York: The Viking Press, 1964.

Helen Diner. *Mothers and Amazons: The First Feminine History of Culture*. New York: Anchor Press/Doubleday & Co., 1973 (1929).

Sir Arthur Evans. *The Earlier Religion of Greece in the Light of Cretan Discoveries*. London: Macmillan and Co. Ltd., 1931.

Lewis R. Farnell. *The Cults of the Greek States.* Oxford: Oxford University Press, 1907.

Marija Gimbutas. *The Goddesses and Gods of Old Europe, 6500–3500 B.C.* London: Thames & Hudson, 1974; Berkeley: University of California Press, 1974.

Robert Graves. *The Greek Myths.* Middlesex, England: Penguin Books, 1961 (1955).
The White Goddess. New York: Farrar, Straus and Giroux, 1966 (1948).

Roland Hampe and Erika Simon. *The Birth of Greek Art.* New York: Oxford University Press, 1981.

M. Esther Harding. *Women's Mysteries, Ancient and Modern.* London: Rider & Company, 1971 (1955).

Jane Ellen Harrison. *Mythology.* New York: Harcourt, Brace & World/Harbinger Books, 1963 (1924).
Myths of Greece and Rome. London: Ernest Benn Ltd., 1927.
Prolegomena to the Study of Greek Religion. Cambridge: Cambridge University Press, 1922 (1903).
The Religion of Ancient Greece. London: Archibald Constable & Co. Ltd., 1905.
Themis: A Study of the Social Origins of Greek Religion. Cambridge: Cambridge University Press, 1912.

E. O. James. *The Cult of the Mother-Goddess: An Archaeological and Documentary Study.* New York: Frederick A. Praeger, Inc., 1959.

C. G. Jung and C. Kerenyi. *Essays on a Science of Mythology,* translated by R. F. C. Hull. New York: Pantheon Books, 1949.

C. Kerenyi. *Zeus and Hera*, translated by Christopher Holme. Princeton: Princeton University Press, Bollingen Series 65-5, 1975.

G. Rachel Levy. *The Gate of Horn: A Study of the Religious Conceptions of the Stone Age and Their Influence upon European Thought*. London: Faber and Faber Ltd., 1946; Atlantic Highlands, New Jersey: Humanities Press.

Spyridon Marinatos. *Crete and Mycenae*. New York: Harry N. Abrams, Inc., 1960.

Friedrich Matz. *The Art of Crete and Early Greece*. New York: Crown Publishers, Inc., 1962.

Patricia Monaghan. *The Book of Goddesses and Heroines*. New York: E.P. Dutton, Inc., 1981.

George E. Mylonas. *The Hymn to Demeter and Her Sanctuary at Eleusis*. St. Louis: Washington University Language and Literature Series, No. 13, 1942.
Mycenae and the Mycenaean Age. Princeton: Princeton University Press, 1966.

Erich Neumann. *The Great Mother: An Analysis of the Archetype*, translated by Ralph Mannheim. Princeton: Princeton University Press, Bollingen Series 47, 1963 (1955).

New Larousse Encyclopedia of Mythology, 1968 Edition. London and New York: The Hamlyn Publishing Group Ltd., 1976.

Martin P. Nilsson. *Greek Popular Religion*. New York: Columbia University Press, 1947 (1940).

A History of Greek Religion. Oxford: Oxford University Press, 1949 (1925).
The Minoan-Mycenaean Religion. New York: Biblo and Tannen, 1971 (1950).

J. D. S. Pendlebury. *The Archaeology of Crete.* New York: W. W. Norton & Co., 1965.

H. J. Rose. *A Handbook of Greek Mythology.* New York: E. P. Dutton & Co., Inc., 1950 (1928).

Philip E. Slater. *The Glory of Hera.* Boston: Beacon Press, 1968.

Merlin Stone. *When God Was A Woman.* New York: The Dial Press, 1976.
Ancient Mirrors of Womanhood: A Treasury of Goddess and Heroine Lore from Around the World. Boston: Beacon Press, 1984 (1979).

Elmer G. Suhr, *The Spinning Aphrodite: The Evolution of the Goddess from Earliest Pre-Hellenic Symbolism through Late Classical Times,* New York: Helios Books, 1969.

George Thomson, *The Prehistoric Aegean.* New York: The Citadel Press, 1965 (1949).

Emily Vermeule. *Greece in the Bronze Age.* Chicago: University of Chicago Press, 1964.

R. F. Willetts. *Cretan Cults and Festivals.* London: Routledge and Kegan Paul, 1962.

Gunther Zuntz. *Persephone: Three Essays on Religion and Thought in Magna Graecia.* Oxford: Oxford University Press, 1971.